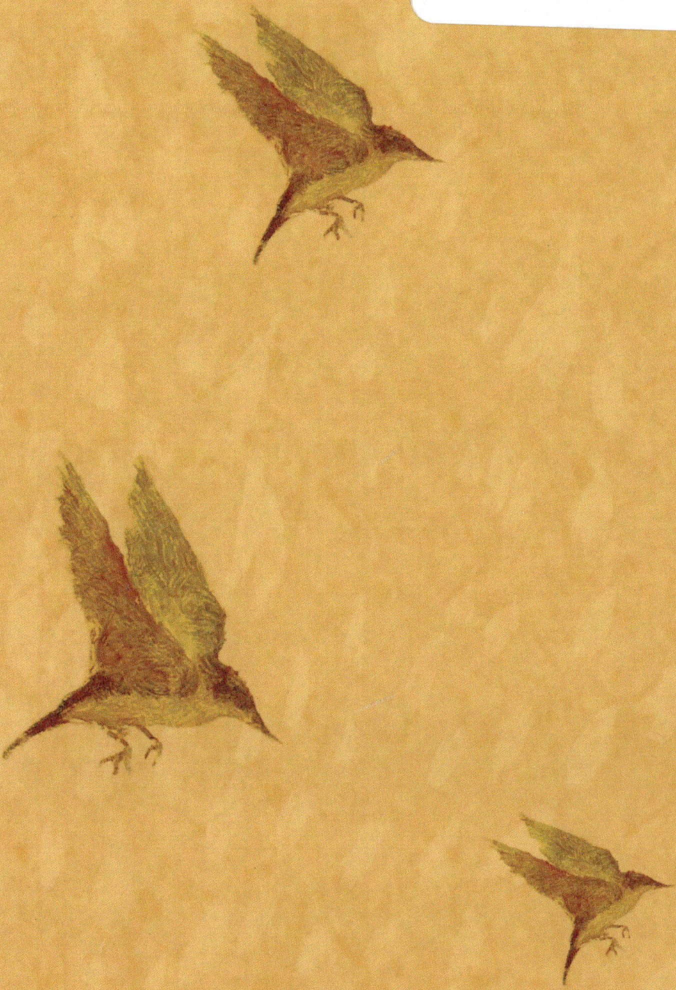

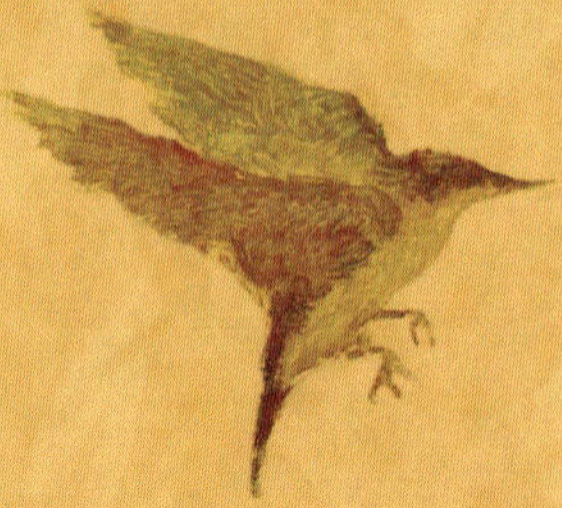

The Obscure Substance *of* Sky

The Obscure Substance of Sky

Alicia Wirt-Fox

CODHILL
PRESS

Codhill books are published
by David Appelbaum for Codhill Press

codhill.com

THE OBSCURE SUBSTANCE OF SKY
 First Edition.

Published in the United States of America

ISBN: 978-1-949933-17-8

Cover and Book Design by Alicia Wirt-Fox
afoxcreativestudio.com

For all those
who live in-between

Contents

The Obscure

Substance

Of Sky

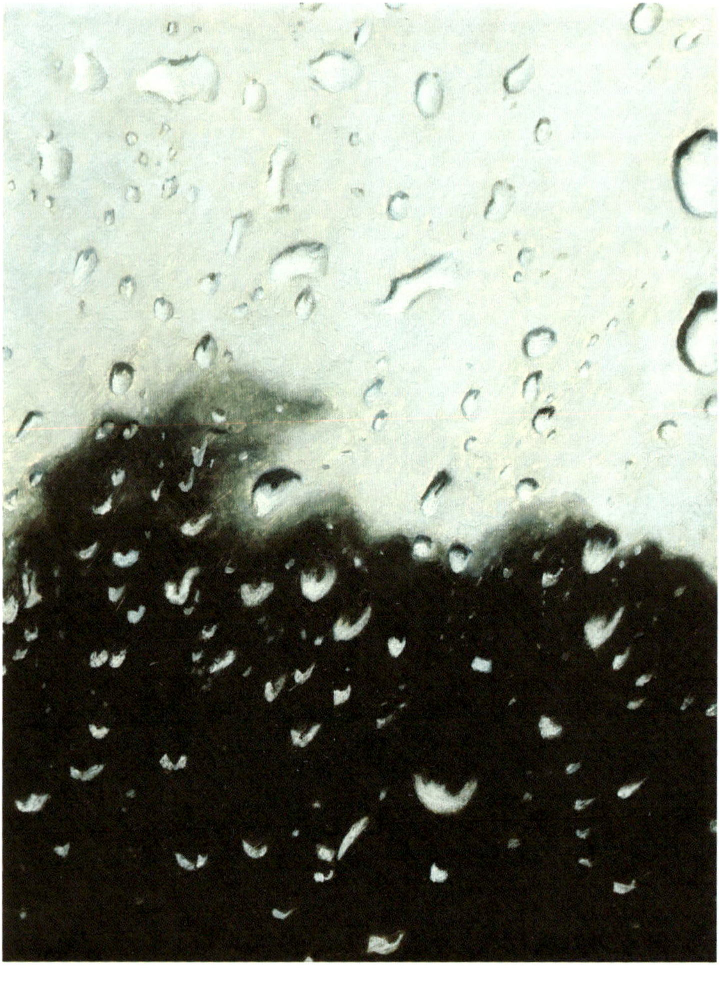

The Obscure

Flow

for black

Black is fluid
        with movement full and wide—
Etching dryness with its dampness,
        impregnating the open.

As tears well in eye's lowered lid,
        concealing the revealing
                of the open—
Black flows.

A thick, dark stream
        carrying suffering seed
Implanted in the heart—
        in the open.

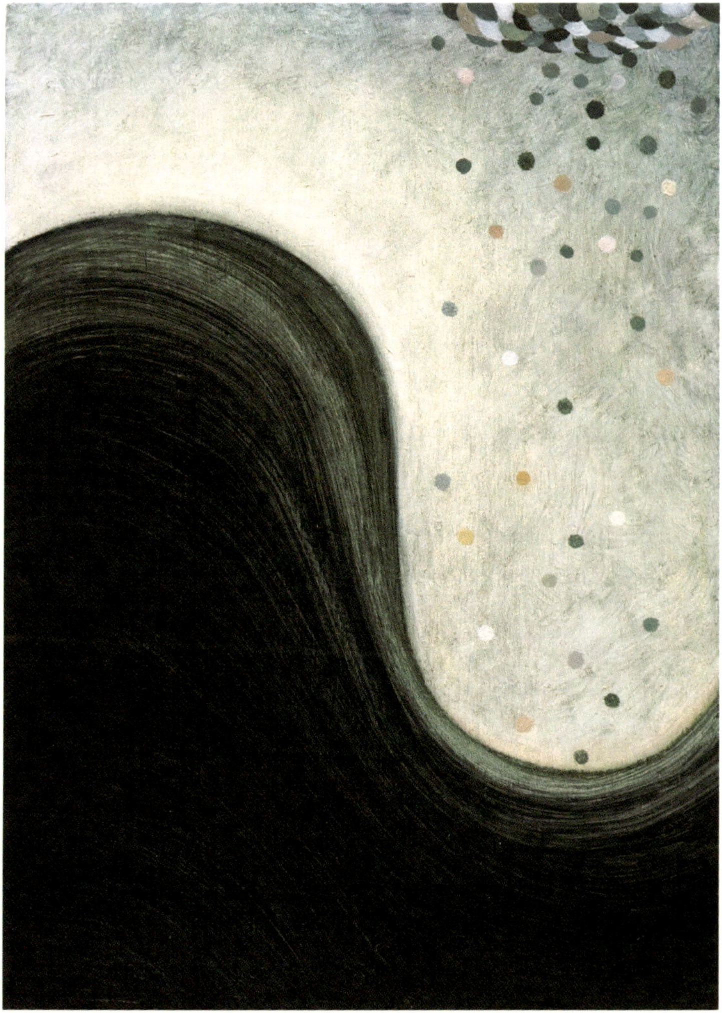

Heartless

Skin abraded
by ceaseless friction
forms a barrier.

Shielding the touch
from nerve.

Blotting out contact
with the living.

A residue created
by ignorance.

Our soft vulnerable skin
turned to stone
by heartless repetition.

Callous.

Volume

Words lead one into another and another and another.
Muzak-like where cheap talk glides upon the surface
        with smiles and lies.
Endless repetition of the same song, same sound, same word.
Saying nothing really,
        really nothing—
                with volume.

A counterfeit caring where exchanges overlap,
        words crossing this way and that.
Saying nothing,
        with no hesitation or regret.

Manacles around my vocal folds
        guard the true and soft down deep.
Wit or tale gloss the glib.
Managing the dead zones with a meaningless drone.
Saying nothing really,
        really nothing—
                with volume.

A True Story of Inexistence

I once tried to get rid of nothing.

But in order to get rid of this nothing,
I had to put nothing   into   nothing.

This second nothing contained absolutely nothing already.

And yet, it was attached to   something.
Did this make nothing into   something?

Now that nothing had nothing in it,
        I put nothing into the trash.

In hopes that the administrators would find nothing
        and delete it.

I awoke perplexed the next morning wondering:

"Had I lost something?"

Negative

A sheet of carbon

Used

Containing a negative
of script

Words that went
somewhere

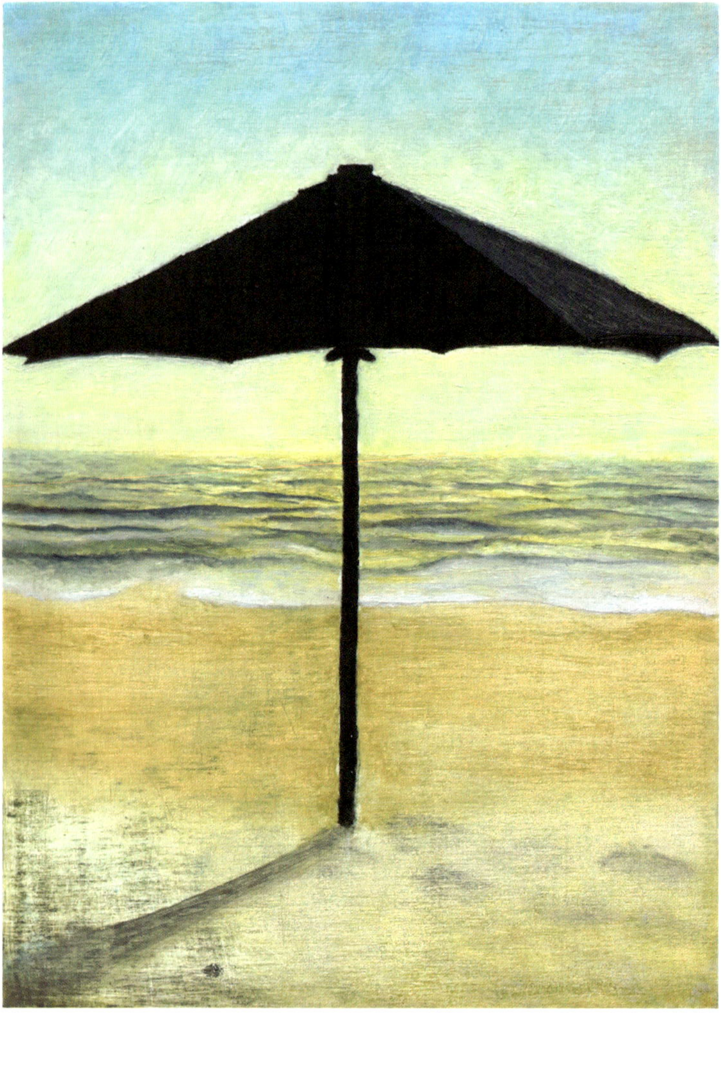

Rockaway

Hot sand burned my feet as I walked to the sea.

Burying the pole of the umbrella
I sat under its shadow
elongating.

People cooled in the waters
becoming shadow form.

Pushed by golden waves
they moved volitionless,
oblivious to the sun.

There is nothing going on here—
and yet,
I am here.

Like a prayer
carried on the wind,
flags flutter.

Spineless

Amicable smile minus warmth.
Regulating, calculating, insinuating,
Control.

Pre-registered response.
Fixed and fixed again.
Advance knowledge prevents
        the pain of waking.

Fragile fake—or is it fake fragile?
Don't know, don't care.
Don't lie.

Intimacy reveals a small, soft mollusk—
No shell,
No protection,
No spine.

Poison is the chosen defense—
The lie, the cheat, the game.

Held at arms length,
All is fair play.

Avenue of the Americas

Walking down the "Avenue of the Americas,"
        I was jostled.
I had taken great pains to avoid them,
        the people I mean.

You know—
        The ones that smoke,
                that smell funny,
        The ones who speak loudly to their "friends"
                or to other disembodies entities,
        The others with strange dress
                or fashion sense,
        Or those that simply annoy with a look or glance,
        The fat ones, the poor ones,
        The ones that I'd rather not be
                if I had a choice,

But here is where I stopped.

I had avoided and did not see, because
        they were me.

                How could this be?

Starling

A reconciliation
hangs between
the trough and crest.

Lacking weight
                    or height
                              or breadth
                                        or depth.

As the light upon
the starling's wings reveals—
                                        everything.

Little beak
ingesting snow crystals
on my windowsill—

Nothing left
          but, exaltation.

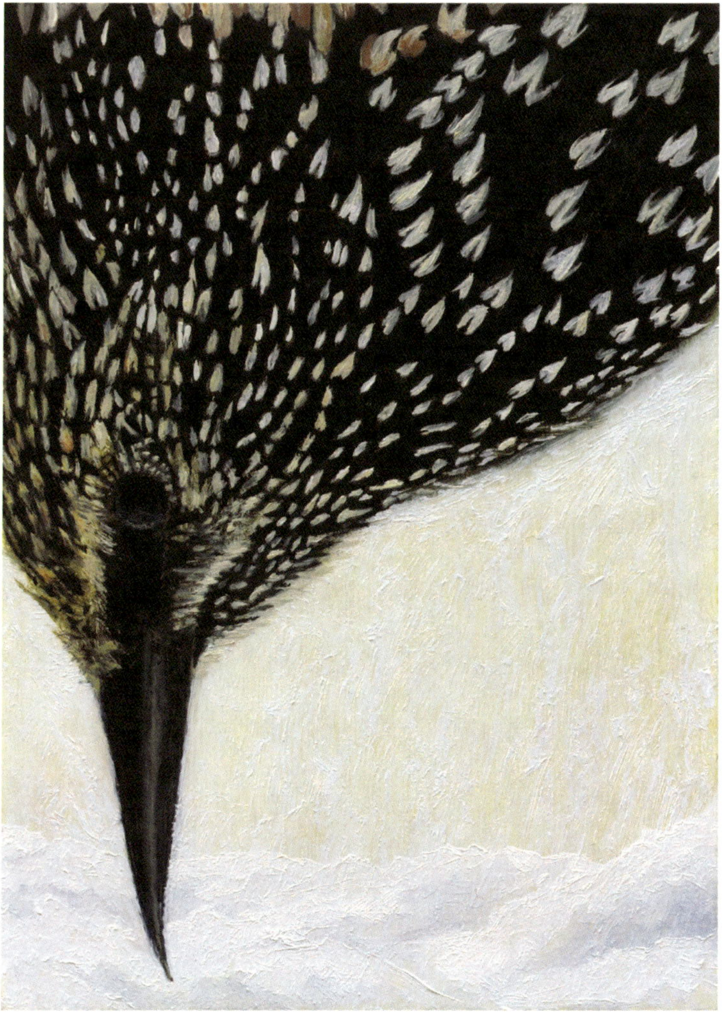

Link

for Dhruvi and Manish Acharya

A ramshackle life I lead
Minced away by time's indifference
Caring only for that single thread
A line of hope

Linking

Margins

for my father

The margins of memory
hold encapsulated moments.

Freeze dried morsels
to be digested when
the time is ripe.

In the clasp of two hands
a message is encoded—
in the palm
in the blood
in the nerves
in the heart.

Messages set in the margins
connected by a
thin
blood-red
line.

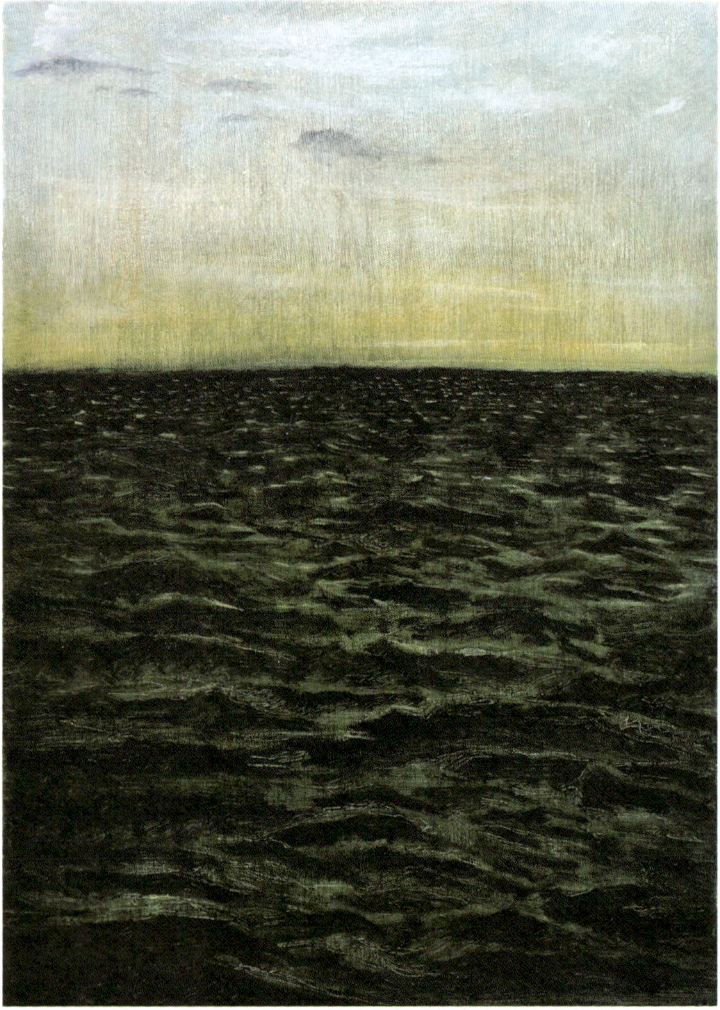

Undertow

Dark waters move.

Silted clouds guide the way
        to delineate the current
                and evoke
                        the direction.

How is it that
we do not see   do not hear   do not touch   or taste
        the evocation?

It is only in the opening
        to void of thought,
                        or knowing
                that we by miracle
        sense the Way
                        in the undertow.

Pulled toward
the shining sea—

I beckon thee,
I beckon thee.

Verge

On the brink

I wait

For a shimmer,
a glimmer,
a sound

I wait

Poised
to receive
that which
is yet to be

I wait

Without despair,
or hope

I wait

On the verge

Flies

I speak of the surface
and the words
have no weight.

They drop
as dead flies do
while falling in flight
having lost
what once tethered them
to the air.

That life in their buzzing,
in their zig zag meander,
steered by desires
for raw, dead meat
and dung
left beside the path.

Their tiny lives living
on what's left behind.

Rejuvenated
in the underworld.

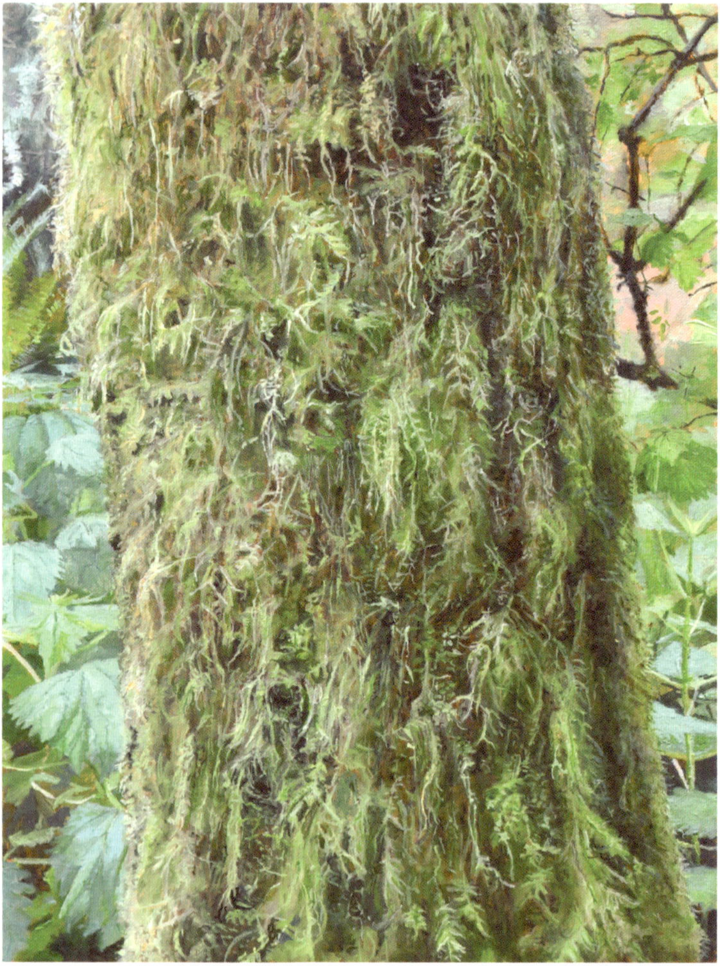

Substance

Underskin

Underneath this skin
I wear another

More porous, voluptuous
invisible and free

Possessing
magisterial ease

Directing my movements
from beneath

I bend to uncover
its form

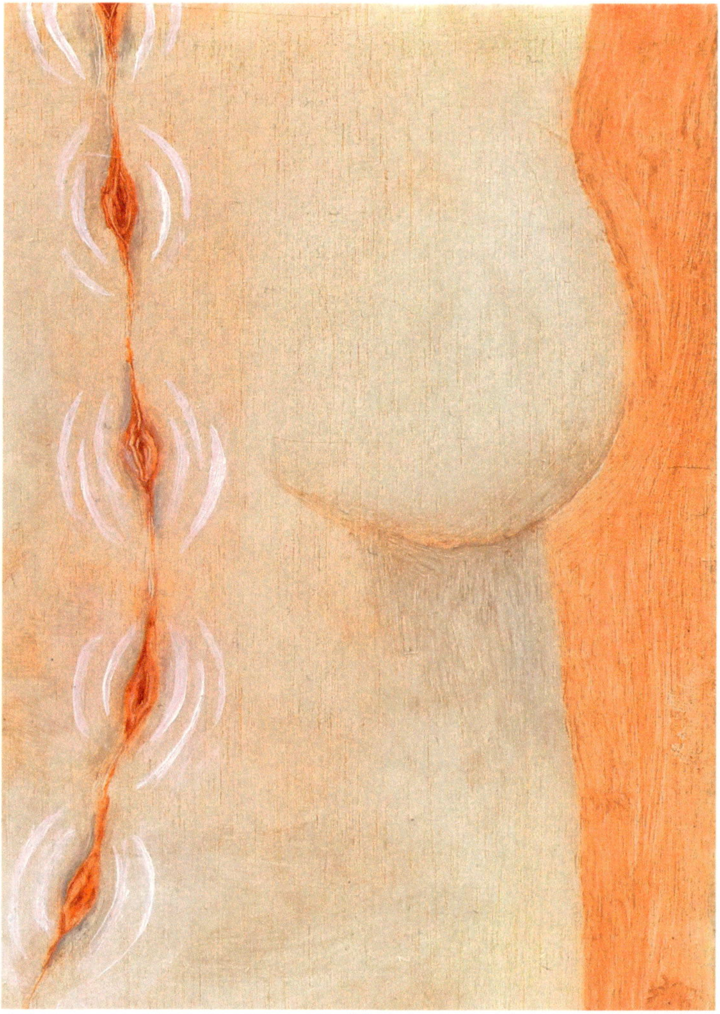

Bell

Upon awakening, or
was it half sleep?

My body was struck by a mallet
and its sound rang out in the quiet.

Accompanied by the
awareness of death and life,
being no place,
                    no where,
                              everywhere
in sound.

I was silence sung in a moment—

          Struck—

my body singing like a bell.

Substance

soft sky
dark mother
has hidden form

no reflection
no revelation

and still
I am received

cradled   hushed

I fall upward

each singing star
a sibling

my pores embrace
the sound that
forms us, shapes us

lending us its substance

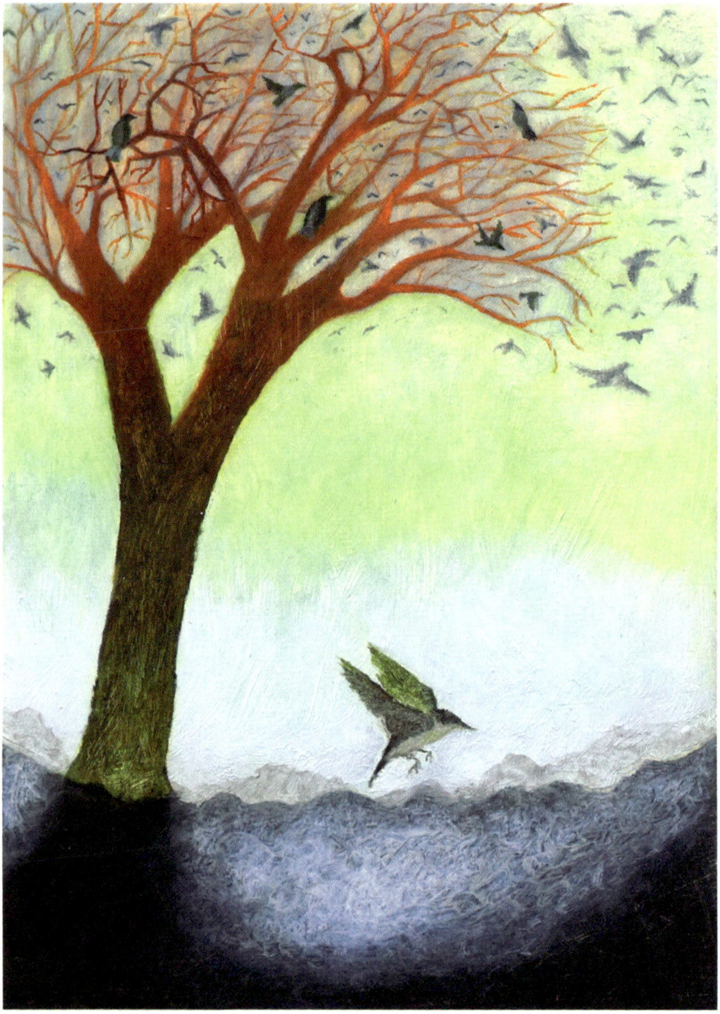

Travelers

I stand to watch
as travelers perch
merging with the invitation
of outstretched limbs.

Their small light bodies
shimmer,
shivering in the haze
of gray morning.

It's just an instant
that they wed themselves
to the web of winter wood.

Warming the sap,
fostering the reaching
red glow of new branching.

Life undifferentiated.

I too am wedded
for an instant—
watching as they part,
never to return
the same.

Fibers

A stalk of
        fibers stretched

The receiving tubes of
        whispering sound

An undulating word
        half heard
        marking time

Its undercurrent
        pulls me
        down
        into cradling soil

To wait
        for radiance

And re-emerge a stalk of fibers
        stretched

Lockdown

underground
the dirt surrounds
my burrow

comforting

my soft belly
detects the pulse of Earth
tendrils of fur unfurl to
sense, reaching

She is weak

gasping under
the burden
of the creatures
who have forgotten

our bodies reliant
        on Her breath, Her blood

how to stay within?

The Path

The ground of Earth
welcomes each footfall
upon the entry way to Spring.

A long cold winter, not far
from memory,
        and shed in pine needles—
as humid earth absorbs my weight and form
in endless forgiveness.

Feet sensing sweet softness of
the Mother of us all.

She welcomes each regardless
of our incapacity
to see her need of us.

And we, insensitive
to her touch,
do not recognize
her continual acceptance.

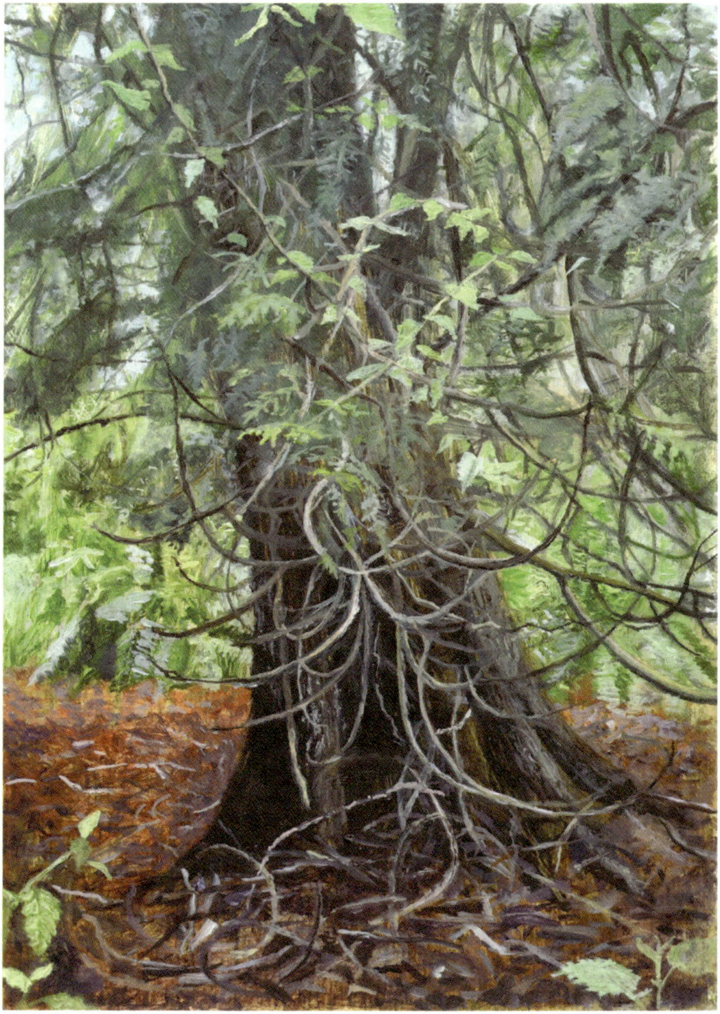

Words

The body clenches to grasp
the last word coveted by
mind's meagerness.

Seeking
palliative resolutions
concretized in an utterance
from a ghost.

Phantoms hover
in the guise of dust clouds—
        molecules taking
        shape for a time.
Some longer,   some not so long
        and resting in memory—
                believed.

Hypnotized by seeming
        solidity.

Utterance

A syllable tethered
to my entrails
abides half way
between my chest and throat.

It simmers
then seeps into
my molecules
dissolving into still finer bits
to radiate through every pore
until it shows in skin and eyes.

Eventually it is
                    undeniable.

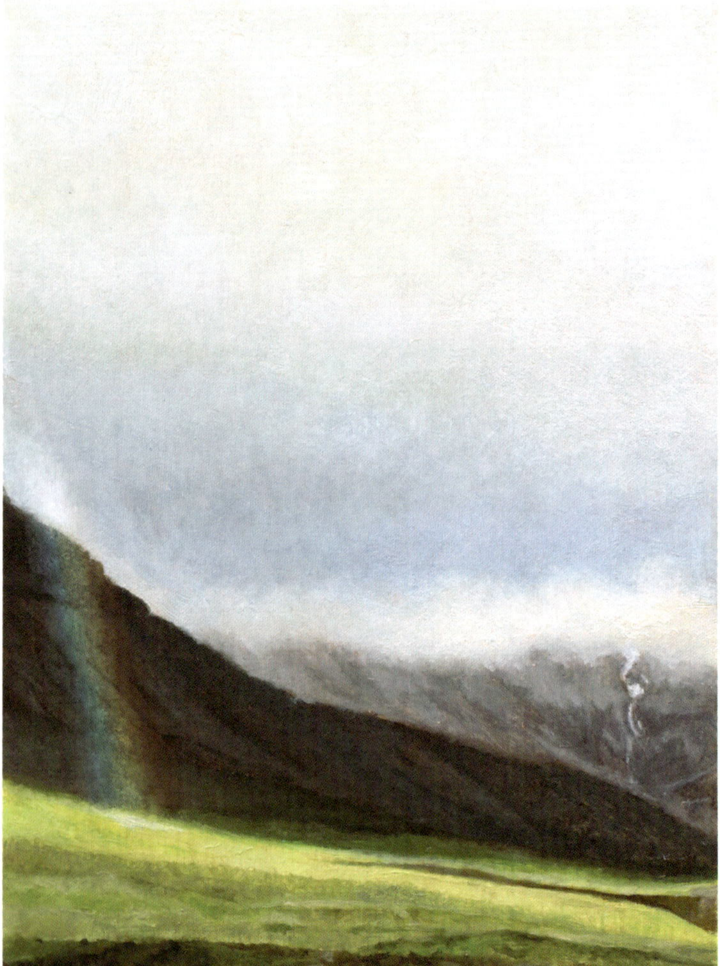

The Arc

Both ears
hear
the arc of an
undulating conveyance—
carrying a beginning,
an endless beginning,
of being singing itself.

I live this cascade of sound.
I am this cascade of sound.

And in this miraculous instant
where I am no longer—

I accord.

Dissolve in endless beginning.

Drops

The drops descend
one by one
markedly, deliberately,
with benevolence.

And trust to be received
wholeheartedly,
by the One who dares to love.

The drops descend
one by one
easing the way open
markedly, deliberately.

To prepare the One
for the torrent
of grace yet to come.

The drops descend
one by one to compose
One's tears of love in kind.

Enough

The heart has no location

Except when there
        are two

And in-between
        it comes to rest
for a moment

Something

Spring
        is messy—
gray grass
        bedraggled,
ancient stems
        hallow.

Now waiting
        to be plucked away
by the beak of
        feathered parents.

At least they serve
        something.

Noticed

I never noticed
my branching plant—
the choices it makes
to extend an arm
toward space.

Does each bud calculate
its chance to ingest
the sun?

Or is it enticed forward
by warmth
to draw its form?

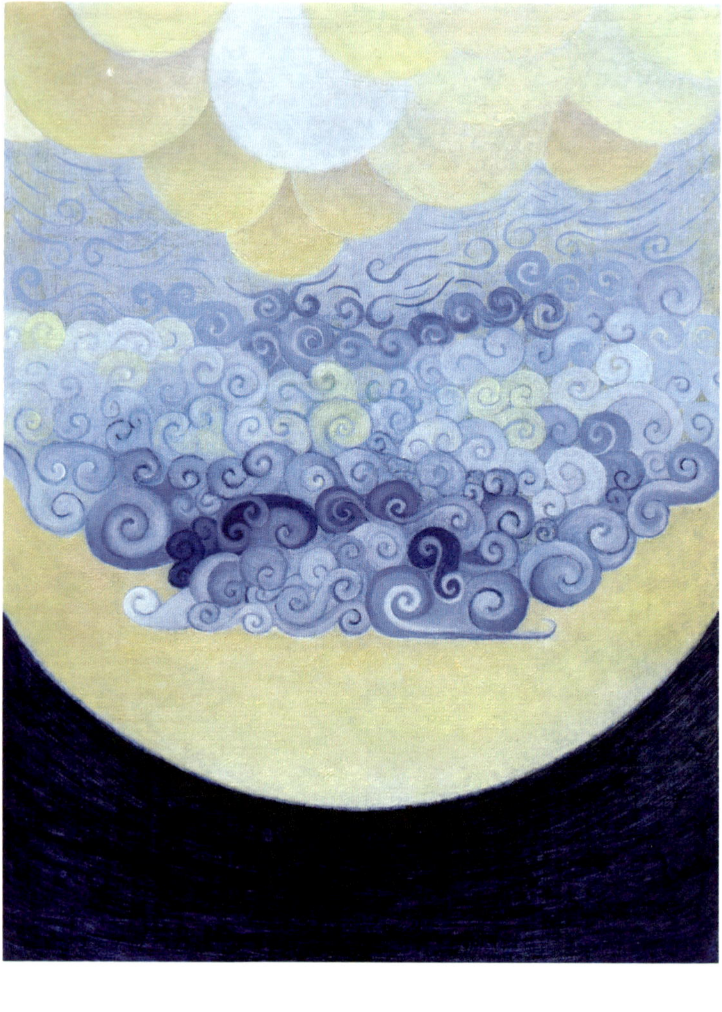

Of
Sky

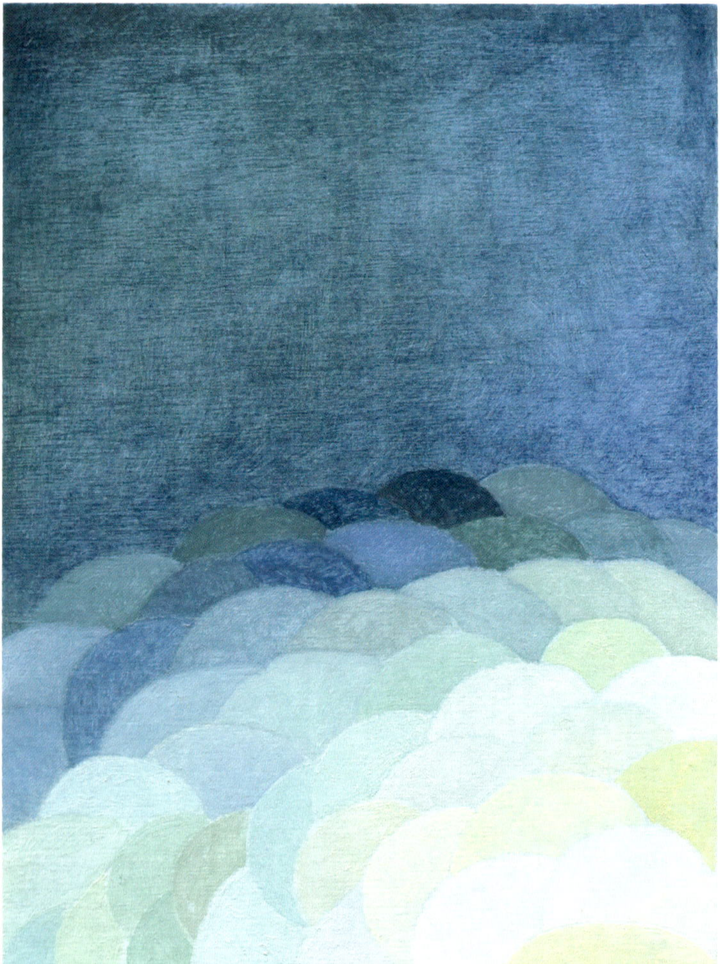

Endless

For Blue

Blue is empty
endless
light.

I absorb it through my pores,
my nerves.

All my tendrils extend
to meet its coming arrival.

I drink it in rhythm
through the core at the center.

Expanding and contracting
with its far-ness and near-ness.

Child

A cloud of light descends.

Revealing that I am neither here,
nor there.

But have transformed into
a bright white liquid
streaming down
from stars and sun.

My skull an empty sphere,
my hips a waiting bowl,
and my spine serpentine
stirs this liquid line.

Spinning this stream
into a shining orb.

A child of stars and sun.

Heliotrope

Silt carried by
a mournful wave
passes, passes.

I am covered in its aftermath—
a dull grey coat worn to honor
the dead.

Nothing to do, but wait and see.

So I sit under the open sky,
to sip each drop of light bestowed.

I watch, as each gritty particle
of dusty memory takes flight
effervescently.

My body mirrors
the sky—
and I, like a heliotrope,
am finally free to obey
my beloved sun.

Mountain

I stand
before the mountain
and I am hushed.

A space opens.

And everything
that I once call myself
                    escapes.

No longer captive
I listen, I wait.

Absorbed into
the sound of the mountain,
                    a river descends.

Love
is that
and does not
discriminate.

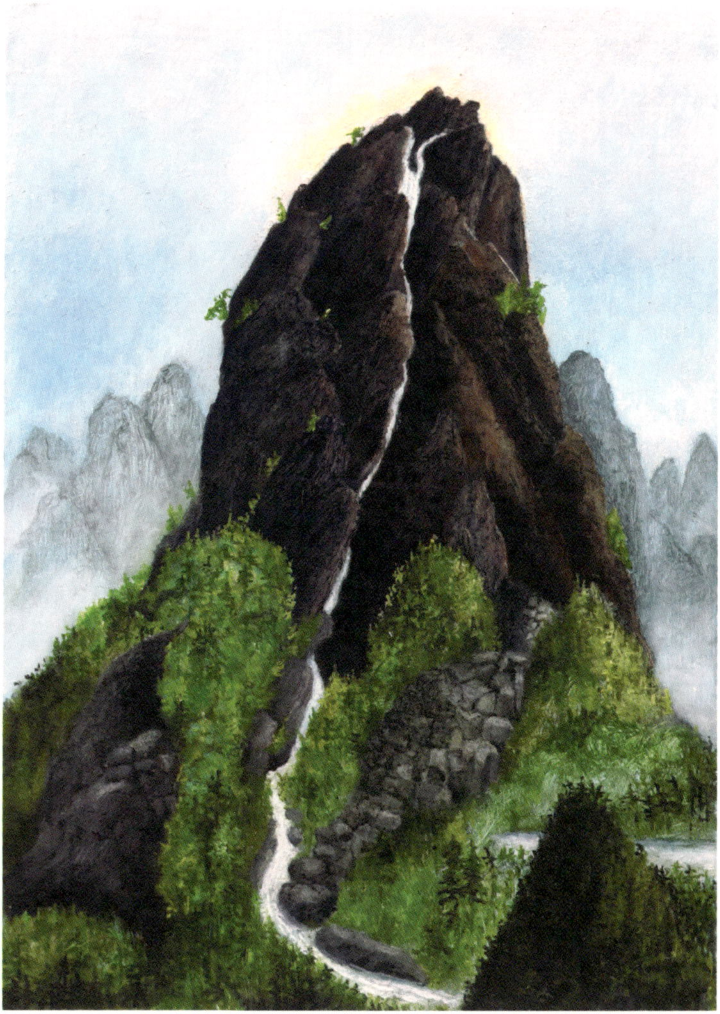

Sky

Grasp the wind
Grasp the river
Grasp the sky
Grasp the you and the I
    the sunlight
    the life
    the sea
Grasp this movement
    inside of me.

Oh we try
    and try
        and try!
and yet we find no end
to the flow
        of fluidity.

Proof

for Yunus Emre

proof of an open heart
is undeniable
when nothingness
loves everything
for no reason

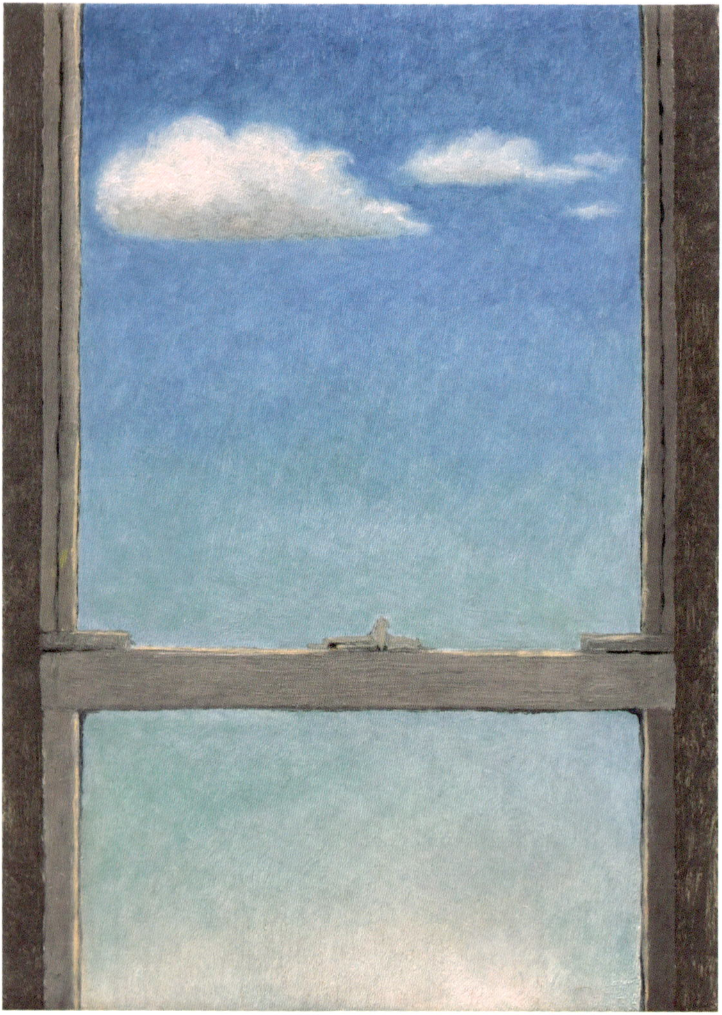

Left Behind

I look around for a thought
to begin
and there are none.

Not a word.

I watch as wisps of grey cloud
pass above.

Space is so precious
and we forget that it is always here,
dangling.

Sometimes I feel left behind
and wonder why it's so.

On Visiting Agnes at the Guggenheim

for Agnes Martin

My underbelly drinks in the surface
pores suck in light
the whisper of winds
far above
hit tree tops

    My mind is swept.

As she brushes me away
draws me away
with a single line
reaching beyond
my periphery

    Revealing my blindness.

Testing my capacity
to be happy
and remain
close
to the soft undulations
that hang in the air
like angelic hymns

    I receive elation.

Painted ladders
ascend
to the land of light
where angels
scrutinize my coarseness

and I
    draw near
        perfection.

To My Friend

One day gazing up into the bluest of blues
I saw a something
small and white, drifting...

It was so far, so small in size
a glimmer to my eyes
just a speck of bright white, drifting...

No form could be distinguished
just a movement,
twinkling, star-like, drifting...

Is it governed by will
or currents whim?
It spiraled,
circled, drifting...

Then another joined in jest
and put my query to the test
"It is will and whim", I guessed.

They spiraled, circled, drifting...

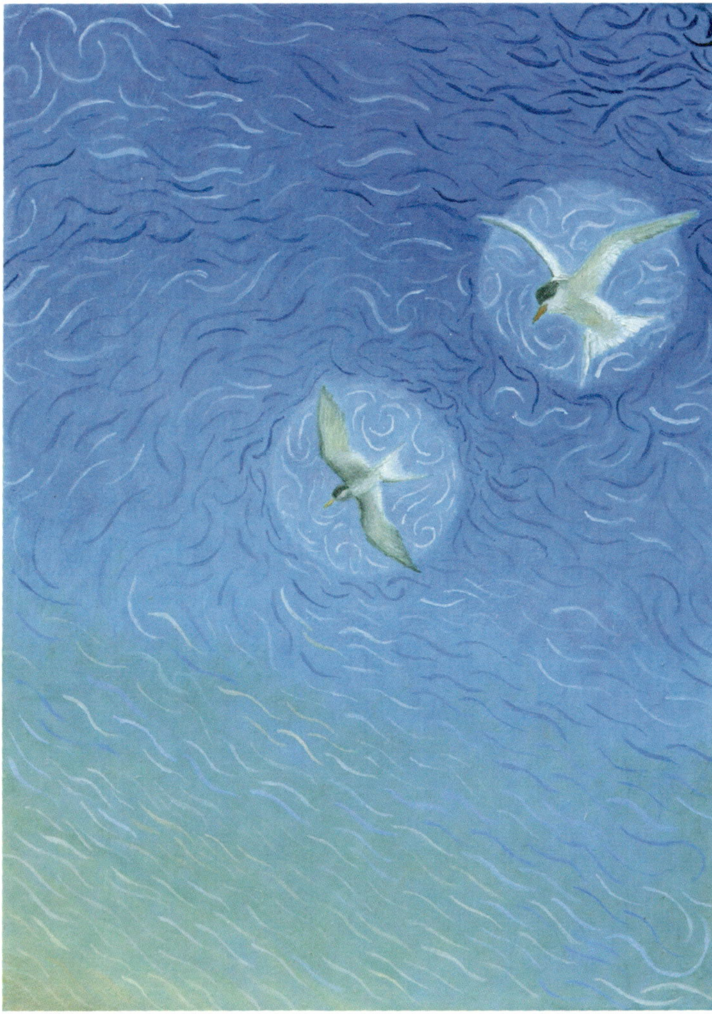

Instrument

A hollow waits for
a passing breeze
to give it voice.

Suspended above us,
it whispers soft hymns
inaudible to my coarse ear.

Defying the tangible desires
of my lesser part.

It avails itself to this undetected miracle
and is instilled with a sound
that purifies our living.

Counterpoint

A point above
a shining drop
of that veiled light
only felt when its
counterpoint
is known below,
a mere reflection—
yet radiating nevertheless
with as much efficacy.

And when I sense and see
with other eyes and skin
a secret sphere appears
to envelope both in tandem.

And you and I
likewise
are contained
therein.

Stowaways

Words emerge slowly from beneath.

Sounds inclined this way or that way,
luring me to the outside,
urging me to produce concrete syllables with
prefabricated meanings.

All these articulations seem alien to me.

Borrowed sounds—rearranged, juxtaposed and stretched.

Carry in-articulated meaning underneath,
stowaways unseen, unheard—
deposited upon arrival.

To be received by a stranger who knows at least their names.

Raptors

for my teachers

We inhabit spaces in-between
        the vast distances of mountain peaks,
where raptors fly on soft air currents
                and guide each feather
toward a place   unseen,   unknown,   unheard of,   ever.

        I do not remember my home.

Mind desolate, inconsistent.
        Readily evaporated
                        in an instant.
It doesn't matter,
                it has no matter
of fluidic movement
        distant.

Resonating the interstices
of a substance eternal.

The medium of Word
tunes us
unceasingly, in question.

Between the Between

A life notated
in detail
spoken
in retrospect
misses the dirty streets
and tedious moments
waiting at stop lights
the moments that pass
walking down a frozen sidewalk
between stores at a shopping mall
or the moment
where one
needs to
bend a knee
to tie one's shoe.

We say:
        get on with it!

and forget
        what is
hidden
        between the between.

As a young child,
I used to dance in the vestibule
between the staircase and the front door
in the house where I grew up.
And the day
my mind was opened
happened there.
Time stood still for an instant
and my eight years of existence
were called into question.

Breathless
I was thrown
between the between

Each night when I sleep
silence pours down
to awake
with a gasp

Born once more
between the between

Not

I revel in the news
of the becoming

In the becoming
that always was

Never missed
nor forsaken

Never found

Never sought
in imagined
sweetness
or solemnity

Hum

This hum, delicate
fluttering

A soft receptive
sense
rings in my flesh

Permeates my perimeter
to collect

And recollects
our homelessness

Never settling

About the Author

Alicia Wirt-Fox was born in Chicago, Illinois. She received a BFA from Parsons School of Design in 1987 and an MFA from Yale University School of Art in 1997. Her first collection of poetry and paintings entitled *Missives* was published by Codhill Press in 2009. She wrote a series of poems in collaboration with the photographer Alan Barnett entitled *Blind Date* published in 2012. She is a recipient of the 19th Annual Richard Kelly Grant for her experimental work utilizing reflective light and color within the context of painting. She teaches at the School of Visual Arts in New York City and currently lives and works in Greenpoint, Brooklyn.

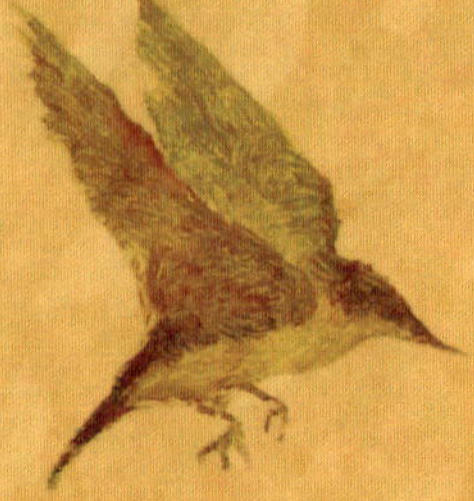